D1809460

[CONTEMPORARY APARTMENTS]

BETA-PLUS

[CONTEMPORARY APARTMENTS]

The kitchen of an apartment on
the Belgian coast designed by Aerts
+ Blower.

4-5
This apartment on the
Mediterranean was created by
Kelly Hoornaert, an interior
architect with Obumex.

$\begin{bmatrix} \text{CONTENTS} \end{bmatrix}$

[FOREWORD]

This book presents 15 apartments recently completed by renowned interior architects. The creation of an apartment calls for a very special approach that often differs substantially from the skills employed to create a house. The interior architect must take into account the limited space, the lack of incident light, etc.

With over 300 unique photographs, this new title in this series of thematic interior design books is a wealth of information for anyone with a contemporary apartment intending to carry out redesign work or do a makeover.

Wim Pauwels
Publisher

A roof apartment designed by Koen Aerts and Roos Blower on a meander of the river Scheldt.

A HOLIDAY APARTMENT
OVERLOOKING A MARINA

This apartment is a typical example of Obumex's international approach as an experienced partner in exclusive total concepts.

Kelly Hoornaert, who works with Obumex as an interior architect, was entrusted with the task of designing and coordinating this project.

This apartment, with its splendid view of the yachting marina on the Med, is the epitome of homeliness and sheer relaxation.
The natural materials and soft colours form a timeless whole, along with a few surprisingly clear works of art for good measure.

The spatial arrangement of the apartment has optimised the available surface area: the areas visually blend into one another but nevertheless maintain their particular function thanks to the use of a different colour scheme, a difference in the floor level or a change in the floor covering.

Desk by Promemoria and chair by
Interni. Spotlights by Delta Light.

The bar was created in dark stained oak with a back wall made of lilac lacquered glass. The fireplace is coated with Zebrano wood with a high-gloss finish.
The chaises longues are by Christian Liaigre.

Dining room chairs and table by Interni.

The kitchen was created by Obumex in dark stained oak.

This bedroom features a white lacquered stool by Bataille & Ibens.

A central stainless steel kitchen block with stools designed exclusively for Obumex by Nedda El Asmar.

The bedroom floor, the washbasin and the shower wall are coated with Golden Brown natural stone. Bathroom furniture made of stained sycamore with washbasin fittings by Antonio Citterio. The bathtub is by Aquamass.

A bed by Lema and a mirror by Maxalto.

In the shower cabinet, grey smoked glass is combined with white Carrara marble.

Obumex nv
Diksmuidestraat 121
B – 8840 Staden
www.obumex.be
T +32 (0)51 70 50 71
F +32 (0)51 70 50 81

A TIMELESS PIED-À-TERRE
ON THE BELGIAN COAST

Interior architect Katrien Van Biervliet designed this newly constructed apartment in Knokke-Zoute.

She was commissioned to create the apartment from scratch, which meant that she could free her imagination to define the spaces and select the choice of materials for the floors and walls, the lighting, etc.

The stylish simplicity, the rather austere lines and the perfect finishing have given this apartment an unmistakable aura of class and serenity.

The sober interior design is a harmonious mix of high-quality materials, subtle colours and timeless furniture.

This apartment offers the owners a pied-à-terre in this exclusive seaside resort.

The fireplace wall was created based on a design by Katrien Van Biervliet. The cupboard fronts are fully finished with matt varnish.
The back and the base of the central recess are made of steel sheet, while the horizontal set of shelves is coated with Wenge veneer. Bio-ethanol fire by Metalfire.
A Busnelli chair is covered with coarse linen.
The poofs, the armchairs and the coffee table are by Promemoria.
The oak parquet floor has been bleached and lime-washed.

Two views from the lounge area to the kitchen.
The entire kitchen was designed and made to measure by Katrien Van Biervliet. The cupboards are finished with painted MDF. The worktop is coated with a composite stone.

Caffé chairs around a Bassano table, both by Promemoria.

The master bedroom with en-suite dressing room and bathroom.
Bed linen by Decopur, lighting by Stéphane Davidts.
The entire floor and shower unit in the bathrooms are coated with white marble mosaic tiles.
Bathroom cabinets finished with matt painted MDF, surfaces made of composite stone.
The standard cabinets designed by Lema were integrated into the bathroom design by Katrien Van Biervliet.

The guest bedroom with en-suite bathroom is once again infused with sobriety.
Cabinets by Lema and bed linen by Decopur.
The guest bathroom with its spacious shower is tiled with marble mosaic. The tailor-made cabinets finished with matt painted MDF give a sense of overall continuity.

Katrien Van Biervliet
Interior Architect
Kleine Kerkhofstraat 133
B- 8310 Bruges
T/F +32 (0)50 345 579
MOB +32 (0)476 29 40 41
www.withuys.eu
katrien@withuys.eu

TAKING IT EASY
IN KNOKKE-ZOUTE

The client bought this apartment in the shell construction phase so that the interior architects Koen Aerts and Roos Blower could experiment with the position of the non-load-bearing walls.

As a result, they could tailor their design work precisely to meet the client's requirements, with the focus on relaxation and freedom from stress!

The kitchen has been moved and has become the heart of the living space. It is fully fitted and practical, but it also forms a central anchoring point with a bar where you can sip a glass of champagne or enjoy an amuse-bouche with friends, a brunch while enjoying a view of the sea…

Around the kitchen block, place has been made for a spacious sitting area and a large dining table where the family can dine at their leisure with friends or the children can play or have fun when it's raining.

The colour scheme and the atmosphere are predominantly white and sober, creating an unmistakable leitmotif around the wide windows that offer a spectacular view of the fascinating coastline of the town of Knokke.

Additionally, the position of the internal walls of the night area has been rearranged by the interior architects in a way that provides each bedroom with a semi-open-plan bathroom.

This enhances the privacy and the sense of relaxation for the parents, the growing children and any guests who may be staying.

This design choice enhances the feeling of spaciousness in the bedrooms.

The long corridor accentuates the longitudinal axis of the apartment from the living area.

To make the most of this space, the wall bench in the dining area has an integrated storage space.

The aged oak panel flooring harmonises with the wet sandy beach.
Thanks to the wide horizontal blinds, the daylight can be filtered as desired.

The partitions of the bathrooms are made of glass. This transparency creates a tremendous sense of spaciousness. The freestanding bathtub creates a separation in the parents' bedroom between the sleeping area and the bathroom area.

Aerts + Blower
Interior and more
Hanswijkstraat 37 A/002
B- 2800 Mechelen
www.aerts-blower.be
info@aerts-blower.be
T +32 (0)15 210 901
F +32 (0)15 210 903

A ROOF APARTMENT WITH A BEAUTIFUL NATURAL VIEW

In the charming town of Sint-Amands, on a meander of the river Scheldt, the team of interior architects Koen Aerts and Roos Blower have designed a roof apartment in a beautiful natural environment that you would swear came straight from the successful Flemish TV series *Stille Waters*.

A conscious effort has been made to keep the design lines and forms sober and restrained.

In contrast, the choice of materials is lavish and natural: white marble from Carrara, walnut and oak, wool and linen.

The night hall is white and sober, with doors integrated in the wall surface and floors made of white Carrara marble.

The kitchen floor and the central block are clad with Carrara natural stone.

The dark stained walnut on the floor of the dining area and the cooking recess finished with black composite stone create a very tasteful black-white contrast.

The kitchen wall, which was purpose designed and built by Aerts + Blower, also features a quasi-invisible pivot door leading to the night area.

The small chairs with their turquoise seats add a touch of slickness and raciness.

The black ceiling in the entrance and the dining area combined with the black curtains, the indirect light and the large suspended lamp ("Skygarden" by Flos) create an intimate atmosphere at dinner time.

An open gas fire separates the sitting room from the reading, working and TV area.
The black walls offer a tasteful contrast to the white furniture, creating an enhanced sense of intimacy and cosiness.
The fireplace hood is made of heat-resistant glass so as not to block the beautiful view of the Scheldt.

The family can read or watch TV while relaxing in the lounge chair, a design classic by Eames which is still in continuous production at Vitra.

The parents' bathroom is extremely sober. The colour scheme is once again predominantly white, with the exception of the wall behind the massive Boffi bathtub, where the interior architects have opted for a classical-modern mosaic by Bisazza.
With the Carrara marble on the floor, the overall effect is contemporary yet luxurious.

Aerts + Blower
Interior and more
Hanswijkstraat 37 A/002
B- 2800 Mechelen
www.aerts-blower.be
info@aerts-blower.be
T +32 (0)15 210 901
F +32 (0)15 210 903

A PANORAMIC VIEW
ON THE 12th FLOOR

This apartment is on the twelfth floor of a new block of flats designed by the Swiss firm of architects Diener und Diener.

The family bought the entire floor (three standard apartments), giving them a 360° view of the entire town.
The basic design was put together in close cooperation with architect Pascal van der Kelen.

A short corridor, of which the walls and the ceiling are completely clad with Spanish oak, leads along a long white wall to the covered terrace between the lounge and the TV area.
A huge enamelled glass panel affords a breathtaking view of the maritime environment.

65-69

The entire surface on the south side, which is between the two covered corner terraces and affords a view of the historic town centre, serves as the lounge and dining room.

Between the lounge and the dining room, a buffer has been purposely created by a low set of bookshelves from the Pascal van der Kelen collection in Spanish oak with a high gloss top. Also, the dining room table made of Spanish oak on a structure of hand polished stainless steel and the light fitting above it made of brown smoked glass are from the same Pascal van der Kelen collection.

The lounge has ideal acoustics thanks to a wall covering made of flannel and a handwoven carpet. In addition, this creates a visual delimitation for the lounge.

The low square table was selected from the Pascal van der Kelen collection.

70-73
The kitchen connects up to the dining room but is located around the corner, on the west-facing side, with a view of a bend in the river Scheldt.
Based on drawings by the architect Pascal van der Kelen, the kitchen was created by Bulthaup using aluminium and natural stone. The same lights were fitted here as in the dining room. As in the other areas, Spanish oak furniture was designed to be peripherally placed here between the windows. This piece of furniture contains books, a hi-fi and the computer and TV screens.

The parents' bedrooms are located on the north side, each with their own bathroom and shower room and furniture made of natural stone, synthetic resin, smoked glass and Spanish oak.
White-painted wooden blinds filter the cool northern light.

The available surface is doubled by the large mirror surfaces.

A view from the parents' bedrooms to and from the dressing room finished in Spanish oak and white wool according to the architect's drawings.

The guest bedroom is on the east side. The wall units and the head of the bed, both made of white painted panels, were selected from the Pascal van der Kelen collection.

Architect Pascal van der Kelen
Britselei 1
B – 2000 Antwerp
www.pascalvanderkelencollection.com
www.pascalvanderkelen.com

SOBER HARMONY IN A CITY APARTMENT

This apartment is located in the centre of Asse and was purchased by the client as seen. The firm of architects Stein Van Rossem designed the interior according to the client's requirements.

The interior designers were commissioned to create an atmosphere that transcends everyday life, exuding austerity and harmony.

Based on these requirements, a single unit was crafted by eliminating all possible excrescences and generating a pure, uncluttered design. All potentially disruptive elements are hidden from view, and emphasis is placed on the aesthetic experience: a pleasant feeling of light, perspective and materials within a tight framework that does not give the impression of being excessively sterile.

The inner partitions without skirting boards have been carefully positioned. The fixed and freestanding furniture was purposely designed according to a minimalist concept. The limited use of materials and the robust details highlight the uniformity of the entire design.

The entrance area is not sectioned off from the living space, an element which enhances the feeling of spaciousness of the apartment.
The ceramic floor, the wall and the ceiling are white, the sofas and the flush ceiling-height door units are made of red stained oak veneer.

The white monochrome living area extends out from the entrance. This area is bathed in light, even on less sunny days. Direct lighting (with "Nude" ceiling spotlights by Modular) is combined with indirect light elements.

An austere L-shaped sofa by Zanotta by the large sliding window with terrace affords a beautiful view of the green cityscape.

The dining area and lounge form one single unified whole. Because of the shape of the apartment, a round table was selected for the dining area.

The tailor-made TV unit and the coffee table, both made of red stained oak veneer, are the focus of all the attention in this "cool white" area. The closed door panels behind the sofa conceal the home office.

84
The shelf and the writing surface of the home office are made of red stained oak veneer. Thanks to the two pivoting ceiling-height white-painted doors, this work area can be closed off.

Extending out from the home office, the open-plan kitchen consists of a wall element that houses all the kitchen utensils and a freestanding block with a high back that also serves as a visual buffer.

The kitchen furniture is made of white painted MDF. The worktops and sink are made of white Corian. Sink fittings by Dornbracht.

The round table, coated with white marble, was designed by Eero Saarinen and blends impeccably into this white interior. The four "Tulip" chairs are also the creation of this Finnish-American architect.

The bed and the bed end were tailor-made and are also made of red stained oak veneer with MDF supports. The indirect light under the bed serves as night lighting.

Like the kitchen furniture, the custom-built furniture in the bathroom is made of MDF and coated with white structured paint. The worktop is made of white Corian with two porcelain sinks by Flaminia. The sink fittings are designed by Dornbracht.

The bath surround is coated with white Corian.

Stein Van Rossem bvba
Edmond Machtenslaan 153
bus 33
B – 1080 Brussels
T +32 (0)2 411 58 51
F +32 (0)2 411 59 51
www.steinvanrossem.be

FROM A DENTAL SURGERY TO A PLEASANT AND COMPACT HOME

The interior architect Filip Vanryckeghem was instructed to metamorphose a dental surgery into a new house.

The need to provide daylight was one of the main problems. Initially, there was only one single large facade window, combined with two roof windows on a flat roof.
Also, the many disruptive construction elements (steel girders, wooden supporting beams, etc.) had to be eliminated, and of course the technical facilities also had to be fully extended.

Filip Vanryckeghem succeeded in putting all the necessary amenities in one single spatial unit, which nonetheless remained very compact.
The carefully designed spatial arrangement of the apartment gives an overall feel of serenity, whereby all the structural elements and the integrated custom-built features blend together to form one single harmonious whole.

The tasteful choice of materials, the warm colour scheme and the carefully selected works of art have created an ineffably pleasant home environment.

The transition area between the entrance hall (on the street side) and the living area (on the terrace side) consists of a volume finished with wood veneer for the guest toilet and the cloakroom. The semi-open-plan kitchen features bar stools designed by Bataille & Ibens for Obumex with kitchen taps by Dornbracht and lighting by Kreon.

The dining room is inseparable from the semi-open-plan kitchen. Purpose-built solid lacquered oak worktop. Oryx chairs by Wildspirit.

The living room (with "Charles" lounge furniture by B&B) forms one continuous unit with the dining area. The two areas are linked by the fitted wall unit (with enough space for a TV, hi-fi, bar, etc.). This is the part of the house that leads to the night area with dressing room/bathroom/bedroom.

The wood veneer wall unit (Alpikord-type) features a wax layer and lacquer work. Painting by Vansevenant.

Works of art by Roger Raveel and Godried Vervisch.

The shower unit in the background is clad with Pietra Piasentina. The bathroom furniture is made of Alpikord wood veneer coated with Corian. Bathroom fittings by Dornbracht.

The guest toilet forms one single unit with the cloakroom. Ciottolo washbasin by Duravit, bathroom fittings by Dornbracht and lighting by Kreon.

iXtra Interior Architecture
Vanryckeghem Filip
Ieperstraat 18
B - 8930 Menen
+32 (0)474-311974
info@ixtra.be
www.ixtra.be

Lucerna 305 reading lamps by Catellani & Smith on an Alpikord wood veneer-coated bed surround.

A PENTHOUSE
IN VINKEVEEN

The design of this penthouse is the fruit of close cooperation between Jos van Zijl and ZETH.

On the client's instructions, Jos Van Zijl designed the different areas of this 350m² apartment. Furthermore, he designed the kitchen, the bathrooms, the relaxation and fitness area, the wardrobe and the glass doors. These tailor-made solutions were also implemented under his responsibility. The design and creation of the entire arrangement was the work of Rob Zeelen from ZETH.

Two parallel skylights provide the living area with abundant daylight.

The Rimadesio Cartesia semi-transparent bookshelf creates a split between the library area and the living room. The Flexform "Happy" chaise longue elements provide relaxation in this area.

Rob Zeelen created the complete sitting area with lounge seating by Cassina and occasional tables by Living Divani on a carpet by Danskina. The curtains are designed by Création Baumann.

The open fire divides the living room from the kitchen.
The high wall of brushed oak cabinets (anthracite) was designed by Jos Van Zijl and combines three functions: living, eating and cooking.
The dining room table is made of solid oak with stainless steel legs. The comfortable dining room chairs are designed by the Italian Baleri. The imposing suspended lamp is by Artemide.

The Byos kitchen crafted with Corian was designed and tailor-made by Jos Van Zijl. The existing elements of the windows (also made of Corian) continue on into the kitchen, creating a monolithic effect.

The guest bedroom is a blend of simplicity and functionality. The washbasins provide space for built-in mirror cabinets. In the shower behind it, extra daylight is provided by a strip of glass that links the columns together. Design and implementation by Jos Van Zijl.

The custom-built wardrobe forms the entrance to the bedroom and the bathroom.

The client's bathroom consists of special tailor-made elements by Jos Van Zijl. He based the design of the granite washbasin and the bath on a monolithic design "cut from one piece".

The wall cupboard unit consists of 35 equal compartments of brushed oak (anthracite) and continues on into the bedroom. The washbasin is integrated in the wall where various user functions have been incorporated such as mirrors, a storage space and a subtle hidden corridor from the bedroom to the nearby office.

The granite bath has a soft cushion that adjusts itself to the body. The built-in Byos head shower has an additional function whereby the rising water vapour is directly extracted while the shower is operating.

Jos van Zijl / ZETH
www.josvanzijl.nl
www.zeth.nl

AN INEXHAUSTIBLE SOURCE OF INSPIRATION

With a 5000 m² showroom, Lacra Lifestyle is one of the most trendsetting and inspiring home design stores in West Flanders, with a wide choice of homemaking ideas and original accessories for your interior.

Craeymeersch Project works closely with Lacra Lifestyle. It has a proven record as a specialist in the total design or makeover of houses, hotels, restaurants, offices, etc.

Furthermore, Craeymeersch Project has for many years specialised in the renovation and (re) design of apartments.
The two projects in this report (pp. 110-115) and the report that follows (pp. 116-121) by interior architect Elke Craeymeersch are striking examples.
All the curtains, wallpaper, furniture, carpets, chairs, etc. were selected from the collections offered by Lacra Lifestyle.

For this Brussels apartment, Craeymeersch Project opted for an open-plan kitchen finished with grey painted MDF and a worktop by Grigio Luna Anciento.
The bar stools are made of varnished Wenge. The curtains are semi-transparent grey etamine.

The central feature is the TV wall (with gas fire, storage cupboard and lounge sofas) painted in "noir de lune".
The galette cushions were tailor-made with linen-cotton fabric (Dott). Quattro canapé covered with grey tweed.
Lighting by Stéphane Davidts and 100% Light.

The console and the dining table were selected from the collection of XVL. They are made of grey stained oak veneer. Poofs and chairs from the Mobitec collection. The orange suspended cupboard is tailor-made and is coated with high-gloss paint.

Namao bamboo living-room table from the collection of JNL in stained Wenge. Grey wool carpet by Ora Pro Nobis.

A Scandix bed from the collection of Nox. Bed linen made of percale cotton. The bedspread was tailor-made. Greige curtains (Dott collection, cotton/linen) on a wrought iron rod. Lighting by Stéphane Davidts, Flamant and 100% Light.

Office and set of shelves in grey stained veneer (XVL). Chair by Mobitec. Curtains made of semi-transparent grey etamine.

Red half-linen curtains (Dott collection) and a turquoise chair from the Mobitec collection in this guest room.

Tailor-made cloakroom cupboard with a seat made of solid roughhewn lye-treated oak. The oak parquet floor with its broad planks was also lye-treated. Flock stripe wallpaper (Flamant) and mirror by XVL.

Lacra Lifestyle – Craeymeersch Project nv
Vlasbloemstraat 2
B – 8770 Ingelmunster
T +32 (0)51 33 29 33
F +32 (0)51 33 29 23
www.lacra.be
info@lacra.be

ONE LARGE AREA FOR COOKING, EATING, WORKING AND RELAXING

In this report, interior architect Elke Craeymeersch (Craeymeersch Project) will again reveal her most creative side, as she incorporates an initially isolated kitchen into a new unit that combines four different functions: cooking, eating, working and relaxing.

A truly inspirational apartment in Antwerp, fully equipped, as featured on pages 110-115, with furniture, fabrics and accessories from the Lacra Lifestyle home store.

The kitchen block is made of MDF, which is painted in greige and coated with sand-blasted Grigio Luna natural stone. Lighting by Modular.
The Milano barstools harmonise perfectly with the red painted furniture and the red leather chairs from the Mobitec collection.

The dining table was selected from XVL's "Longo" collection. The office wall was created with sand-blasted and lye-treated oak veneer. Fil à fil curtains by Nobilis, blinds made of brown leather.

The oak parquet floor is lye-treated.
Canapé made of brown-black leather (Sits collection) and linen/wool carpet by Nash Andrea.

The hall is soberly illuminated with spotlights by Modular. Tennis White paint and custom-built oak veneer storage cupboards (also sand-blasted).

The headboard in the parents' bedroom is covered with white stitch-bonded leather. The wall has grey wallpaper by Elitis ("Glass"). The bedlinen and the stitch-bonded bedspread are made of satin cotton. Curtains and blinds made of white raffia (Dedar collection).

Lacra Lifestyle – Craeymeersch Project nv
Vlasbloemstraat 2
B – 8770 Ingelmunster
T +32 (0)51 33 29 33
F +32 (0)51 33 29 23
www.lacra.be
info@lacra.be

This custom-built box bed made of white painted MDF with storage compartments contains three sleeping units.
Half-linen blinds by Romo and lighting by Modular.

A SPLIT-LEVEL APARTMENT
WITH A MARITIME FEEL

Project Broersbankhelling, which is named after the sandbank in the sea close to this street, is the work of the firm of architects Popeye - Van Landschoot and architect Marc Corbiau.

The entire building is made of concrete and wood.
Concrete was used as the solid base for the two lowest layers of the construction, with wood for the two upper layers with split-level apartments.

These split-level apartments can benefit from zenithal lighting. Thanks to the white-painted walls and ceilings, maximum light is led through a void and the oblique roof terraces, resulting in an impression of unlimited spaciousness.

The wooden wall cladding is a feature that is maintained throughout the interior of this apartment. Teak was used for the floor and the furniture (the buffet, the cladding of the kitchen island, the beds).

D-interior from Moeskroen designed all the fixed furniture.

The use of pale-coloured pebble tiles in the bathrooms completes the seaside atmosphere.

The walls in the bedrooms are also coated with teak wood.

[**PVL**
Popeye – Van Landschoot
Bitterzoetlaan 34
B – 8670 Koksijde
T +32 (0)58 51 48 15
F +32 (0)58 51 53 22
M +32 (0)477 702 373
www.pvlarchitecten.be
pieter@pvlarchitecten.be

A SPLIT-LEVEL APARTMENT AND A BED & BREAKFAST IN BRUSSELS

The team of interior architects Julie Brion and Tanguy Leclercq has completely renovated a typical Brussels house located in the throbbing heart of the Belgian capital.
Their makeover includes a split-level apartment and the resolutely contemporary *Urban Rooms*, which is a bright and airy bed & breakfast.

The variety of functions assigned to the different volumes does not in any way detract from the coherence of the overall design concept.
The interior architects opted for noble materials such as raw timber, lacquered wood and stone.

The designers made clever use of false ceilings to integrate indirect lighting, the ventilation system, the hi-fi, the blinds and the curtains in a way that enhances the purity of the design lines.

The harmony and fluidity of the concept is a perfect example of the holistic architecture approach adopted by the interior architects Julie Brion and Tanguy Leclercq. The result reflects the team's intelligent arrangement of interior spaces, the garden, the lighting, the luminosity and the materials. At the same time, they have succeeded in creating a subtle spatial harmony in their use of integrated and non-integrated furniture.

In order to enhance the harmony of the concept, the architects designed all the interior and exterior furniture, including the 15-seat sofa, the outside bench, the open fire area and the storage units.
A long bench extends the design lines of the dining room and optimises the available space.

The roughhewn wooden table was specially designed and created by the architects.

An immense marble partition creates a separation between the kitchen corner and the dining room, but this does not detract from the sense of spaciousness and transparency that informs the entire design.

The rooms are functional and sleek, with discreet and cleverly concealed storage units.

The bathrooms - created with Carrara marble - are a textbook example of the intelligent use of mirrors to provide natural light and space.

The shared area of the bed & breakfast (the "wake-up room") consists of three integrated table/bench units around an open fire designed by the architects.

Julie Brion
10 rue d'Alsace Lorraine
B – 1050 Brussels
MOB +32 (0)477 32 03 16
www.brionleclercq.com

A CONTEMPORARY APARTMENT IN GSTAAD

Tamara's Design was commissioned to design a weekend getaway home in Gstaad (in the Swiss Alps).

The owners wanted anything but an Alpine interior: the arrangement of the internal spaces and the decoration are purposely very austere and modern for this apartment that the owners occupy mainly at weekends.

The serene atmosphere in this apartment is enhanced by the sense of unity in the choice of materials and colour schemes: the doors, the cabinets and the parquet flooring made of dark stained oak contrast with the monastic white of the walls. Spaciousness was also an important aspect underpinning the creation of this interior.

Tamara's Design opted for black/white contrasts in the living room to ensure optimum airiness and luminosity.
The wall featuring the bookshelves and fire is made of brick, while the recesses are lined with dark stained oak.

Also in the dining area, which forms one single unified whole with the living-room, the black/white contrast is truly striking.
The bench is made of dark stained oak, with panels crafted with tufted white leather.
The table, which also has a dark stained oak surface, rests on a frame made of patinated steel.

The kitchen is rather compact but nonetheless extremely functional. The cupboards have grey lacquered fronts, while the worktop consists of brightly polished Nero Assoluto granite.

In the master bedroom, the walls are covered with white leather panels framed by a dark stained oak structure.
The night tables (also made of dark stained oak) are the creation of Tamara's Design.
The white curtains and the Japanese screen in voile and leather by Elitis enhance the Zen atmosphere of this bedroom.

The bathroom furniture is made of dark stained oak and coated with Turkish limestone. Washbasins by Duravit.

This child's bedroom features square leather wall panels and night tables by Tamara's Design.

This boy's bedroom is awash with black/grey hues. Curtains with a black/grey flannel check motif by Andrew Martin.

Tamara's Design
Interior Architecture & Decoration
Place du Village
CH- 1659 Rougemont
Switzerland
T +41 (0)26 925 94 00
F +41 (0)26 925 94 25
M +41 (0)79 658 10 72
www.tamarasdesign.com
info@tamarasdesign.com

A PIED-À-TERRE FOR BUSINESSMEN IN PARIS

In the Triangle d'Or district of Paris, which is home to many businesses and some of the most prestigious boutiques in the French capital, Gérard Faivre has designed a very up-market apartment.

This high-class project owes much to a traditional concept of sophistication and refinement, but Faivre has added his own personal touch with very contemporary furniture in line with his *prêt-à-vivre* design philosophy.

As soon as you cross the threshold, stylishness is omnipresent: a Cappellini sideboard, a Boffi mirror and a light fitting designed by François Champsaur enhanced by blue LEDs embedded in the false ceiling.

The black is enhanced by subtle lines made with silver leaf by Véronique Chanteau, the artist behind the photograph "La chaise".

The wine rack was designed by Gérard Faivre and created by the Grisard company.

The chairs and the marble table were designed by Eero Saarinen. Sofa by Florence Knoll and painting by the Russian artist Oleg Lang.

The TV lounge (designed by Gérard Faivre) is a tribute to Charlotte Perriand. Two black lamps by Gilles Caffier and photograph by Véronique Chanteau. A vanitas by Krinta Sgourou.

Mirror by Boffi.

Boffi kitchen with rubber floor covering by Nora.

Living room with original 19th-century fireplace. Armchairs by Florence Knoll around a table crafted by Michel Jouannet. Lladro chess set.

Master suite with bedhead by G. Faivre and painting by Claude Barraud. Dedar fabric curtains and chair by Tom Dixon. Cappellini bed by Carlo Colombo.

We see here the corridor leading to the bedroom. Dressing room designed by Gérard Faivre and carpet by Jov.

A 19th-century fireplace lends warmth and style to the bedroom. Vase by Arcade and bio-ethanol fire.

The bathroom is facing the bedroom. Mirror by Bluesky (Langlois-Meurinne).

Boffi bathroom with hammam. Diver by Lladro. Natural stone floor. The painting is the work of the Brazilian artist Kinkas Caetano.

Blue paints by
Ressource.

This bathroom in the guest suite was also designed by Boffi. Curtains by Dedar and black marble floor by Palatino. Photograph by Véronique Chanteau.

The guest suite. Cappellini bed by Jasper Morrison. Painting by Kinkas Caetano.

Console by Monterey and chair by Fonzoni. Cushions by Dedar.

Gérard Faivre Paris
72, rue Bonaparte
F – 75006 Paris
T +33 (0)1 40 46 85 32
T +41 (0)79 528 9755
F +33 (0)1 53 10 84 00
www.gerardfaivreparis.com
contact@gerardfaivreparis.com

A CONTEMPORARY URBAN APARTMENT IN MELBOURNE

This project by Jolson Architecture / Interiors / Landscapes shows a contemporary urban apartment located in Melbourne Australia. Built within the mask of an existing factory shell, the interior spaces are carefully crafted.

The entrance gallery contains a sculptural staircase which is a ribbon of steel which celebrates the transition from the raw and rugged exterior, into a highly refined interior for living.

On the first floor three large rectangular blocks inserted into the space contain and conceal the functional aspects for living to divide each zone: kitchen, living and dining. The kitchen has been fully integrated into the living space and is defined by a black monolithic block of polished stone – the surface selected to carefully maximise 'reflection' of the surrounding flat surfaces and the history of the building. Surfaces have been detailed to create simplistic forms. The second floor contains the sleeping accommodation and bathrooms. The spaces are tranquil layered with a play of natural light, textured surfaces and meticulously detailed cabinetry.

A steel staircase with custom lighting,
integrated handrail and the silhouette of a
David Begbie sculpture projected on the wall.

The sculptural staircase floats like a ribbon of steel in the gallery entrance to the apartment.

Fourteen large portraits line the gallery walls adding vibrant colour to the raw materials of brickwork, steel and concrete.

A Max Mover by Ingo Maurer is suspended like a trapeze above the piano.

This image depicting the history of the confectionery factory conceals the workings of the kitchen which sits as a polished black block of stone.

A B&B Diesis lounge and a nickel Platner table sit on hand woven custom rug from Nepal. The natural timber fireplace is housed in a steel container, with the television descending from a wall cavity above the timber store.

A black Arco Lamp by Achille Castiglioni and the Max Kugler reading lamp by Ingo Maurer provide intimate lighting around the large dining table with Cassina Cab Chairs by Mario Bellini. A steel wall sculpture by the Australian artist Kate Hendry.

The large canvas image depicts confectionery vats belonging to the original space. The artwork slides to reveal and conceal a working kitchen and writing desk.

When closed, the kitchen becomes an integrated piece of furniture.

The kitchen cupboards are constructed from American oak with black Japan stain.

The kitchen sink is carved into the polished black stone. Tap by Supergrif.

The bathroom affords spectacular views of the surrounding city. Stone basins on a low vanity. A black American oak floor.

174
A stone bath on an American oak floor. Image of Pantheon Oculus by Stephen Jolson. A custom designed stainless steel bath rail.

**Jolson Architecture /
Interiors / Landscapes**
58 Greville St
Prahran 3181
Victoria Australia
61 3 8656 7100
www.jolson.com.au

Storage is concealed in the side cabinets, with custom designed full height vertical handles.

176-177
A wood carving by the Australian artist Ewan Ross. A white leather B&B bed with hand blown glass Max Ingrand lamps by Fontana Arte. The dressing room and bathroom are concealed behind.

METICULOUS DETAIL,
A SEAMLESS EXPERIENCE

This luxurious and spacious apartment designed by the office of Stephen Jolson is located in Melbourne, Australia.

The open floor plan living is encased by an L-shaped gallery space which frames spectacular views of the way and coast.

Ebano limestone from North Africa lines the floor and walls of the gallery.

The apartment has been meticulously detailed, with furniture, artwork and lighting being fully integrated to create a play of light and texture, tone and shadow.

Divisions between spaces are created by furniture and cabinets. Each room flows into the next to create a seamless experience. The highly polished stone floors continue the reflective nature of the surrounding water, the hand polished plaster walls allow the natural light to dance into the rich tonal interior spaces.

The apartment contains a large galley kitchen and scullery, a library, gymnasium, three large bedrooms with ensuite bathrooms and dressing rooms, a dining room, a formal lounge, a sitting room, and a gallery.

The main entrance hall floors are lined with
North African limestone, polished plaster
walls and Eames walnut stools.

Framed costal views of Port Phillip Bay in Melbourne. Kreon Lighting and a Rib bench by Stefan Lie.

A Maxalto dining table with Ivory Cab Chairs by Mario Bellini. Max Mover Trapeze lights by Ingo Maurer are suspended over the dining table.

An Alivar screen by Eileen Gray with panoramic costal views.

The open floor plan living with American oak joinery is as a divider between the lounge and sitting room.

An Arco lamp and
Maxalto Simplice sofas on
hand loomed silk rugs
from Nepal.

Dramatic coastal bay views. Knoll Wassily chairs in black leather and a chrome frame.

184-185
Maxalto Simplice sofas
with Knoll Planter side
tables. A custom
American oak cabinet
with a large sliding door
to conceal the bar behind.
Artwork by the Australian
artist Rick Amor.

A custom American oak cabinet with black Japan stain to conceal the television and audio equipment. Maxalto Simplice sofas with a hand-tufted silk rug from Nepal.

The African limestone floor wraps the walls of the gallery space beyond. Concealed lighting is detailed at the wall / ceiling junction. The interior of the bar cabinet is lined with natural American oak as stark contrast to the black Japan stain exterior.

A Carlotta table by Flexform on a Nepalese silk rug. Custom designed raw steel side tables in distance. The limestone floor wraps the walls as textural backdrop.

A floor to ceiling automate white glass door closes to conceal the kitchen. Miele appliances throughout. Concealed scullery kitchen behind.

The galley kitchen with illuminated opaque glass walls. The cabinets and the bench top material are custom made from resin.

The master bedroom suite with an Arca bed by Poliform and Kreon lighting. A hand-tufted silk rug with Cassina Cab Chair.

A custom American oak black cabinet with Gnome by Kartell.

The private gymnasium with Kreon concealed lighting and spectacular Melbourne city views.

[**Jolson Architecture /
Interiors / Landscapes**
58 Greville St
Prahran 3181
Victoria Australia
61 3 8656 7100
www.jolson.com.au

[ADDRESSES]

Obumex nv
Diksmuidestraat 121
B – 8840 Staden
www.obumex.be
T +32 (0)51 70 50 71
F +32 (0)51 70 50 81
p. 14-31

PVL
Popeye – Van Landschoot
Bitterzoetlaan 34
B – 8670 Koksijde
T +32 (0)58 51 48 15
F +32 (0)58 51 53 22
M +32 (0)477 702 373
www.pvlarchitecten.be
pieter@pvlarchitecten.be
p. 122-129

Tamara's Design
Interior Architecture & Decoration
Place du Village
CH- 1659 Rougemont
Switzerland
T +41 (0)26 925 94 00
F +41 (0)26 925 94 25
M +41 (0)79 658 10 72
www.tamarasdesign.com
info@tamarasdesign.com
p. 142-153

Katrien Van Biervliet
Interior Architect
Kleine Kerkhofstraat 133
B- 8310 Bruges
T/F +32 (0)50 345 579
MOB +32 (0)476 29 40 41
www.withuys.eu
katrien@withuys.eu
p. 32-41

Architect Pascal van der Kelen
Britselei 1
B – 2000 Antwerp
www.pascalvanderkelencollection.com
www.pascalvanderkelen.com
p. 62-79

Stein Van Rossem bvba
Edmond Machtenslaan 153 bus 33
B – 1080 Brussels
T +32 (0)2 411 58 51
F +32 (0)2 411 59 51
www.steinvanrossem.be
p. 80-89

Jos van Zijl/ZETH
www.josvanzijl.nl
www.zeth.nl
p. 96-109

PUBLISHER
BETA-PLUS Publishing
www.betaplus.com
info@betaplus.com

PHOTOGRAPHY
Jo Pauwels
p. 166-191: Jean-Luc Laloux

GRAPHIC DESIGN
POLYDEM bvba
Nathalie Binart

TRANSLATION
Belga Translations

January 2011
ISBN 13: 978-90-8944-090-7